Where Does Wind Come from?

Weather for Kids
(Preschool & Big Children Guide)

BABY PROFESSOR
EDUCATION KIDS

Speedy Publishing LLC
40 E. Main St. #1156
Newark, DE 19711
www.speedypublishing.com

Copyright 2016

All Rights reserved. No part of this book may be reproduced or used in any way or form or by any means whether electronic or mechanical, this means that you cannot record or photocopy any material ideas or tips that are provided in this book

It is windy! We can't see it but we can feel its presence. What is wind? Have you ever wondered where the wind comes from?

What is wind? It is a large amount of air in motion, the flow of gases. It is made up of molecules of different kinds of gases. These molecules move in one direction. Wind moves horizontally on the surface of the Earth.

Wind is produced because the surface of the Earth is being heated unevenly. Air is mostly composed of nitrogen and oxygen. The differences of pressure on the Earth's surface cause wind. These differences of pressure are caused by in differences in temperature.

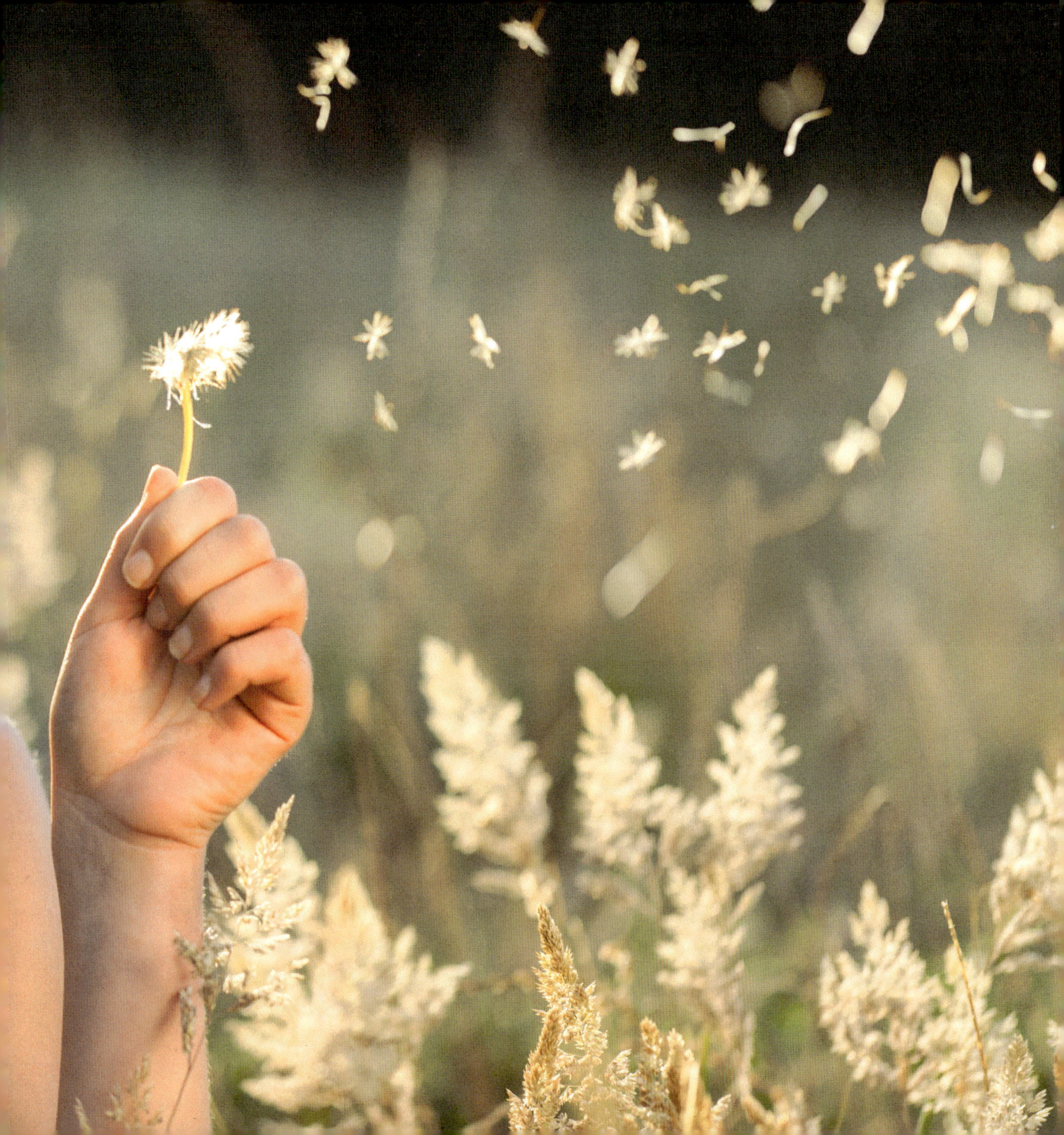

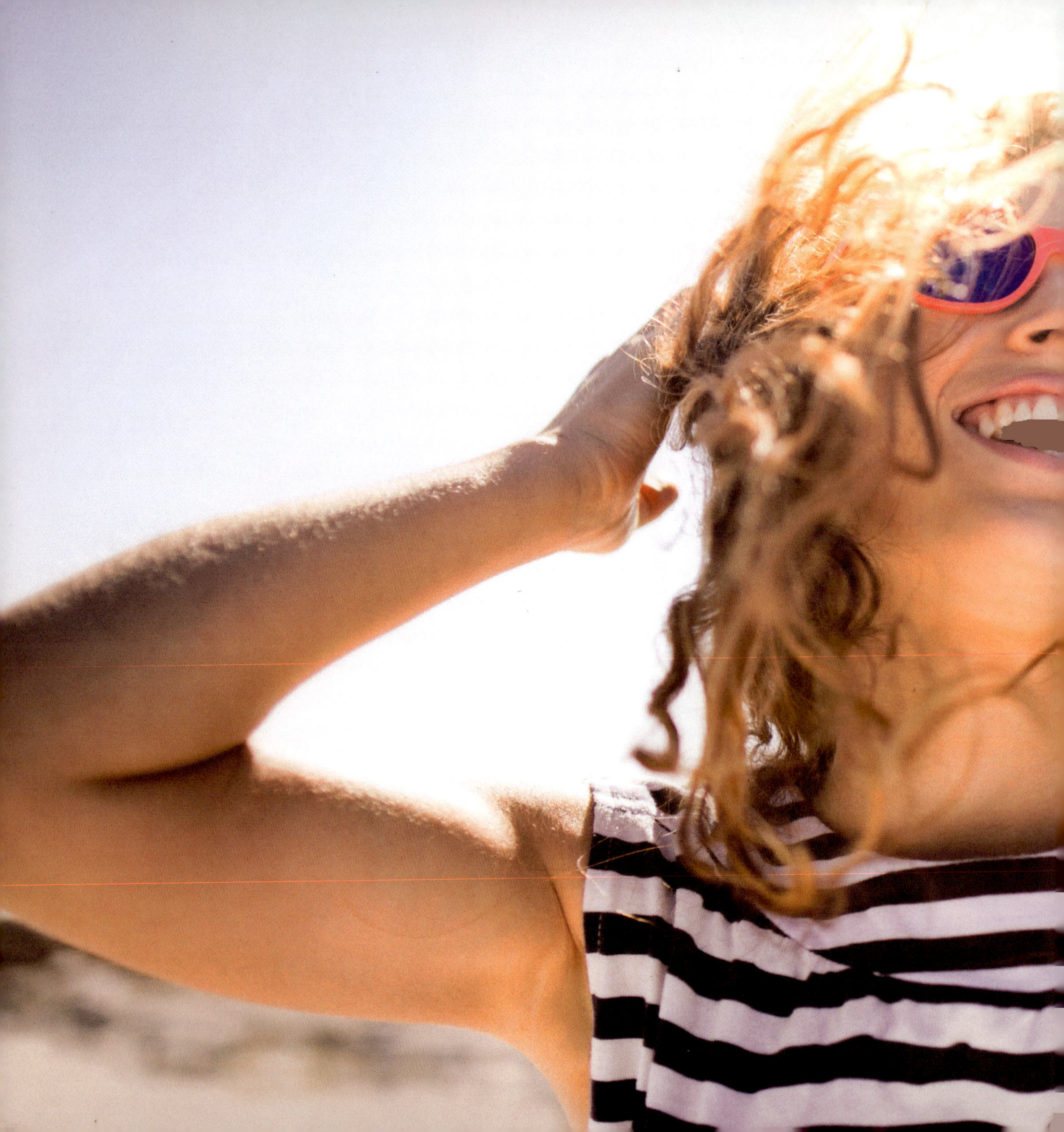

Low air pressure is produced by warm air. High air pressure is caused by cool air. The sun's radiation is spread unevenly on the Earth's surface because of different land and water formations. This causes low and high pressure areas.

The atmosphere gets warm as the sun warms the Earth's surface. Some places on Earth are generally warm for they receive direct rays from the sun. The climate in these places is always warm. On the other hand, there also places on Earth which are colder because they receive indirect rays from the sun.

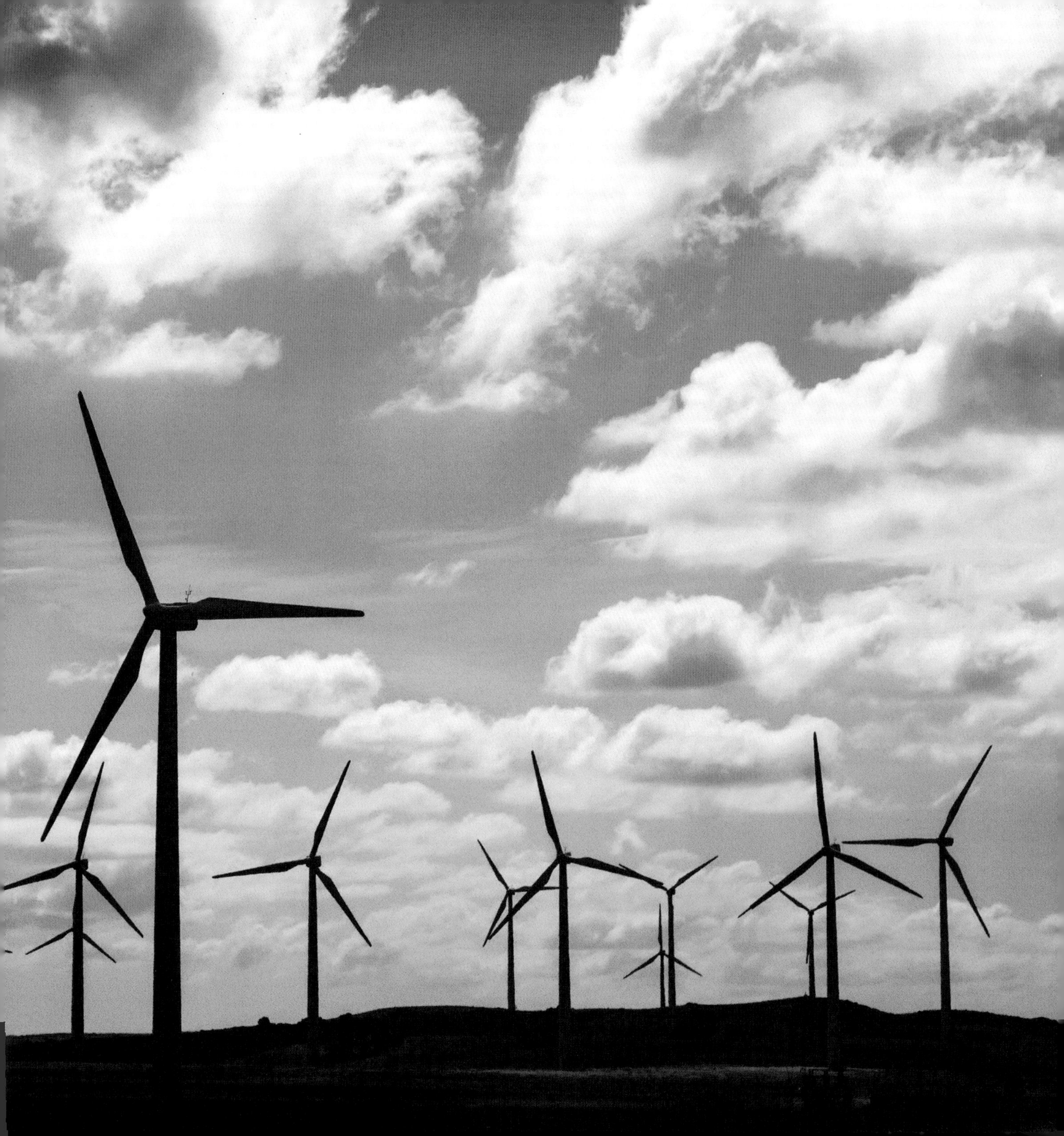

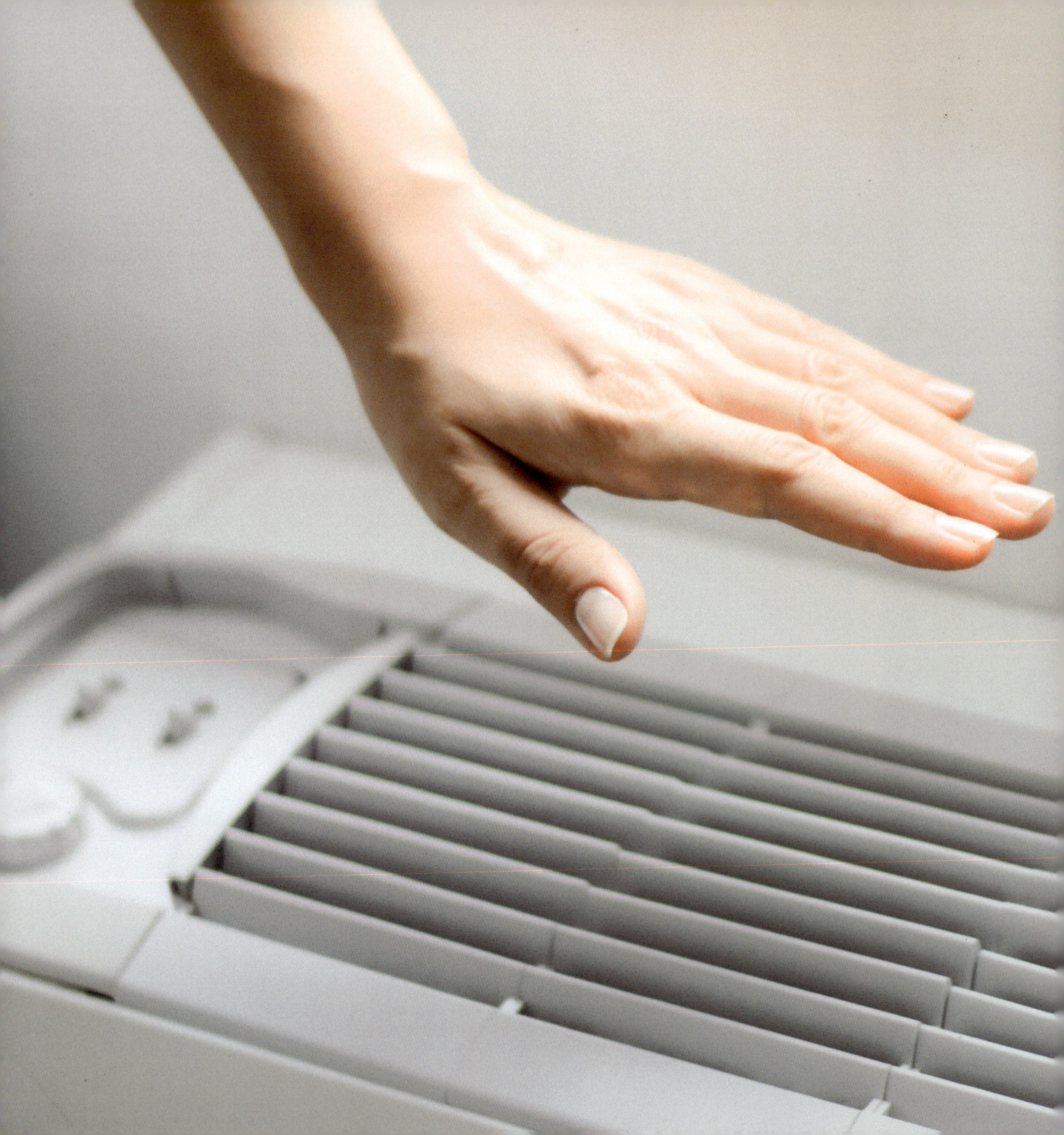

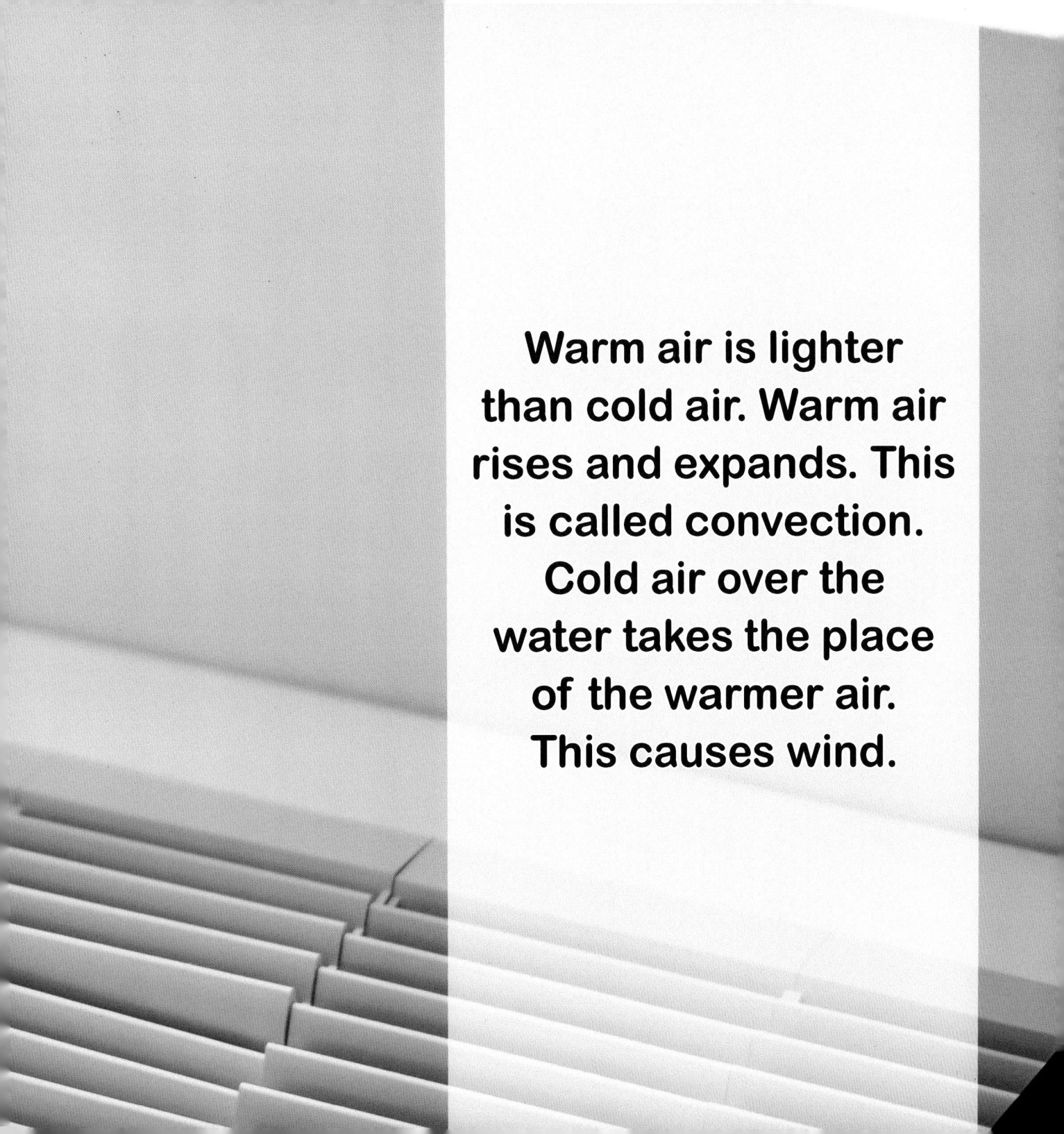

Warm air is lighter than cold air. Warm air rises and expands. This is called convection. Cold air over the water takes the place of the warmer air. This causes wind.

Wind can be described by its speed and direction. These are the two measurements used by meteorologists to describe wind. Air in the low pressure area will move to a high pressure area. When air moves in areas with great differences in air pressure, high winds occur.

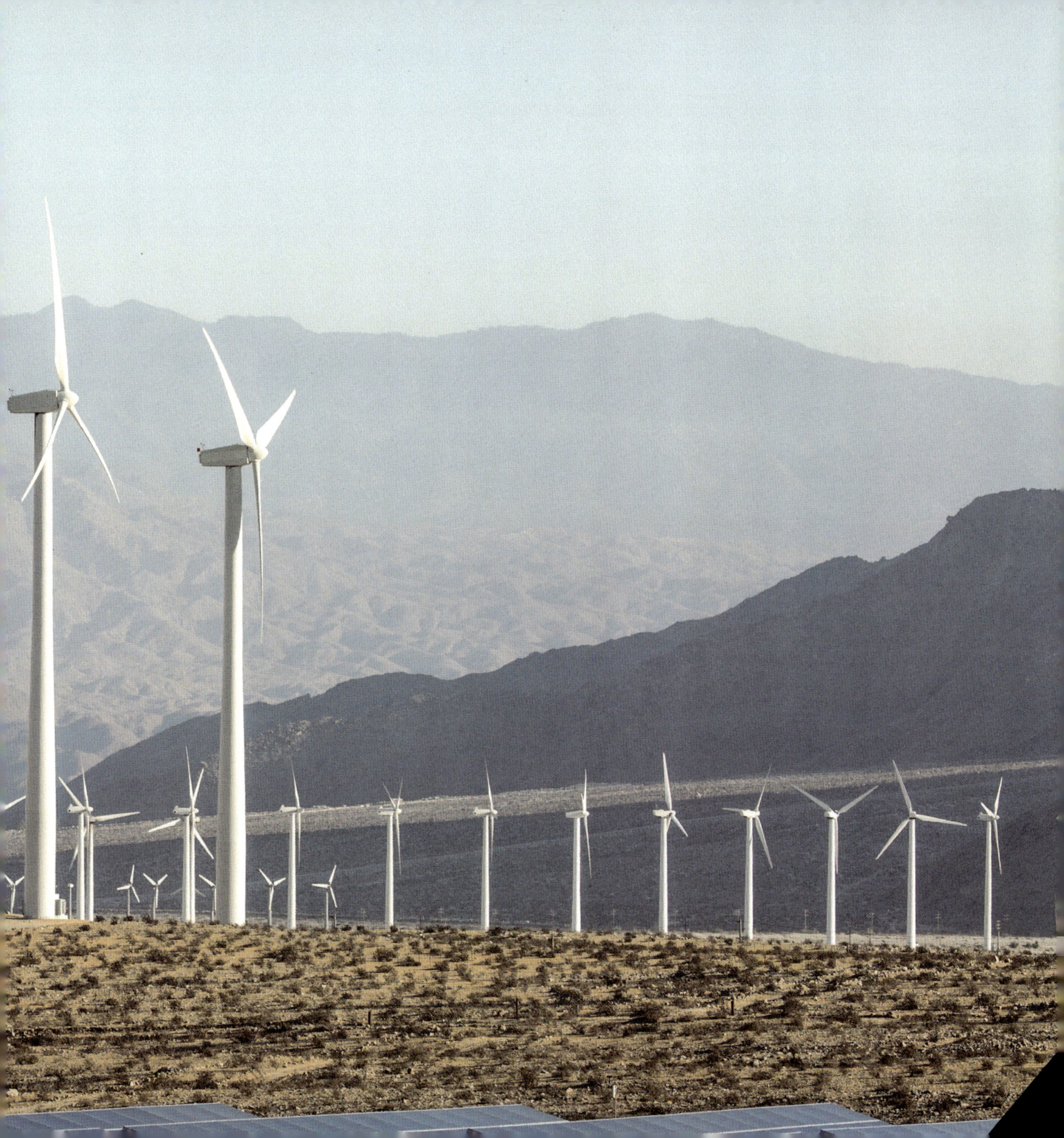

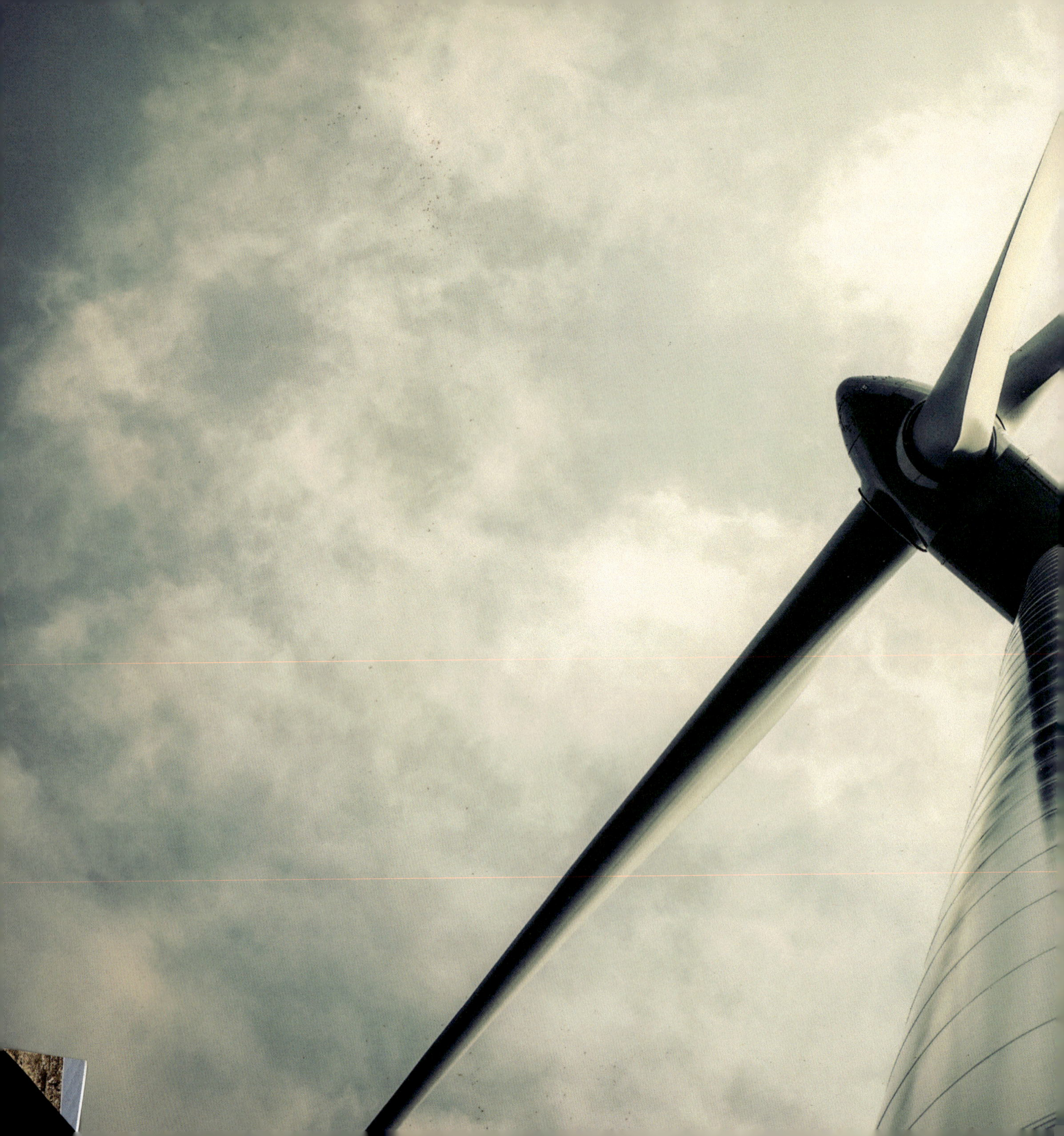

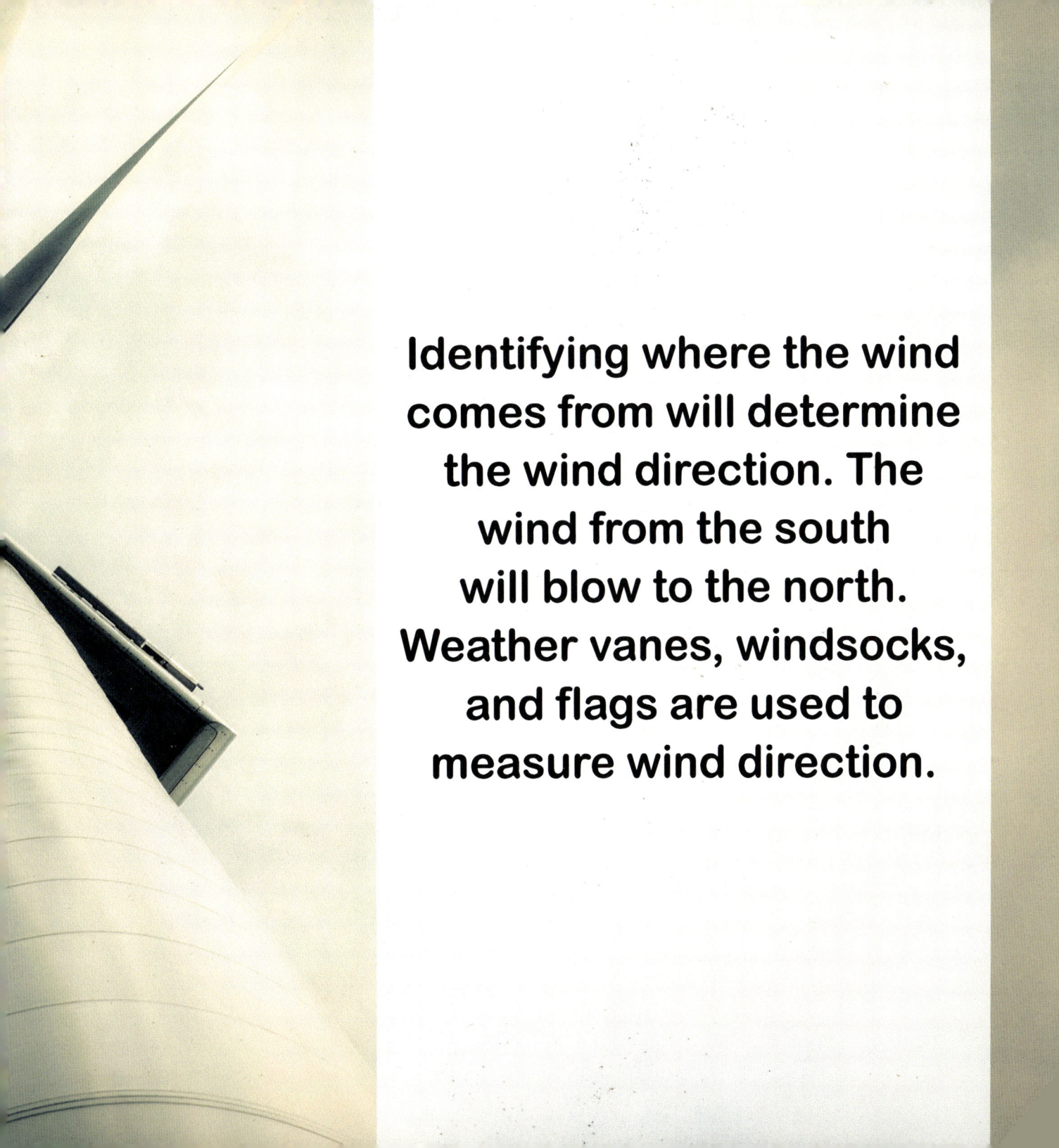

Identifying where the wind comes from will determine the wind direction. The wind from the south will blow to the north. Weather vanes, windsocks, and flags are used to measure wind direction.

The speed of the wind is measured in miles per hour or in kilometres per hour. The speed of the wind is measured using an anemometer.

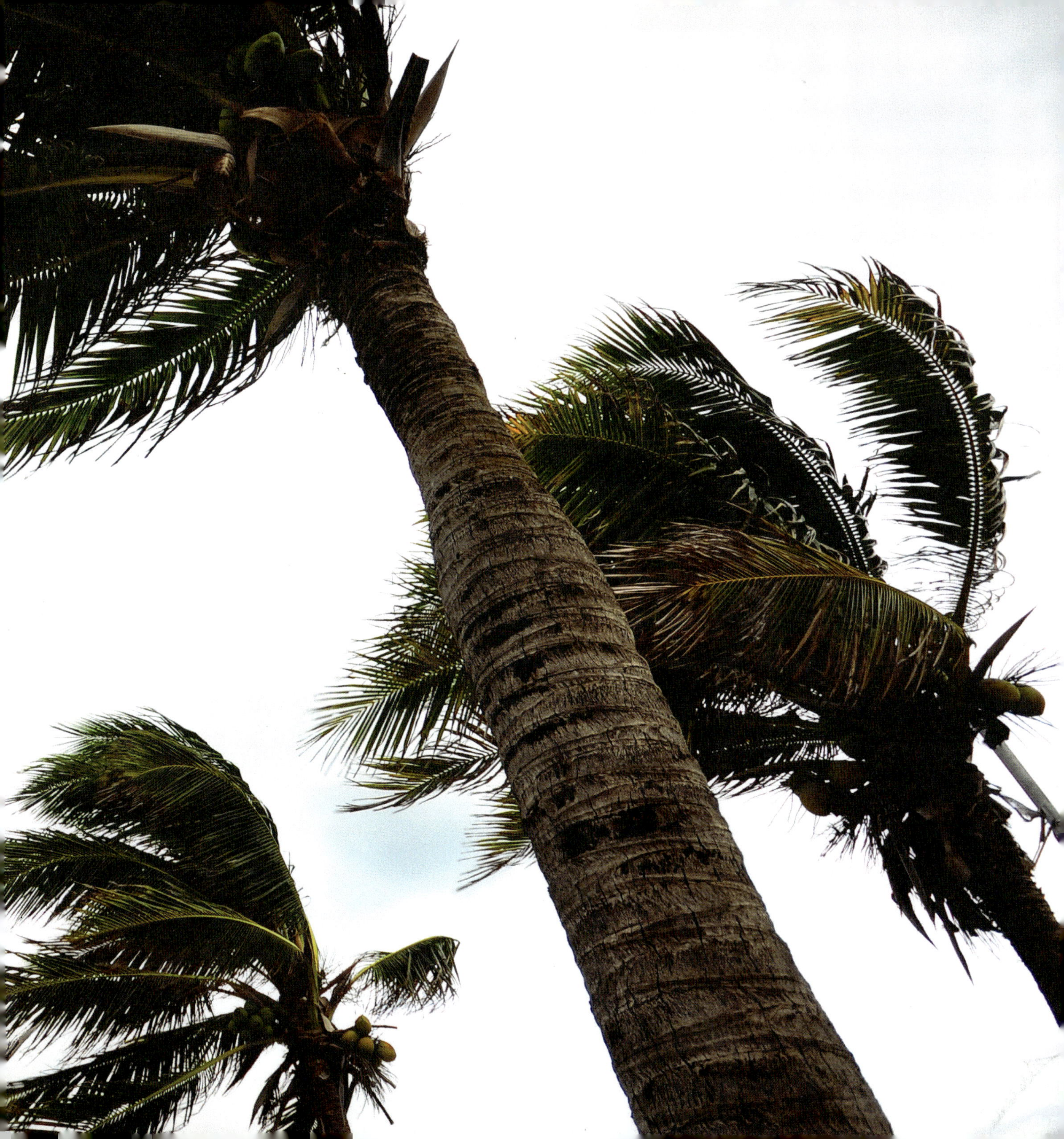

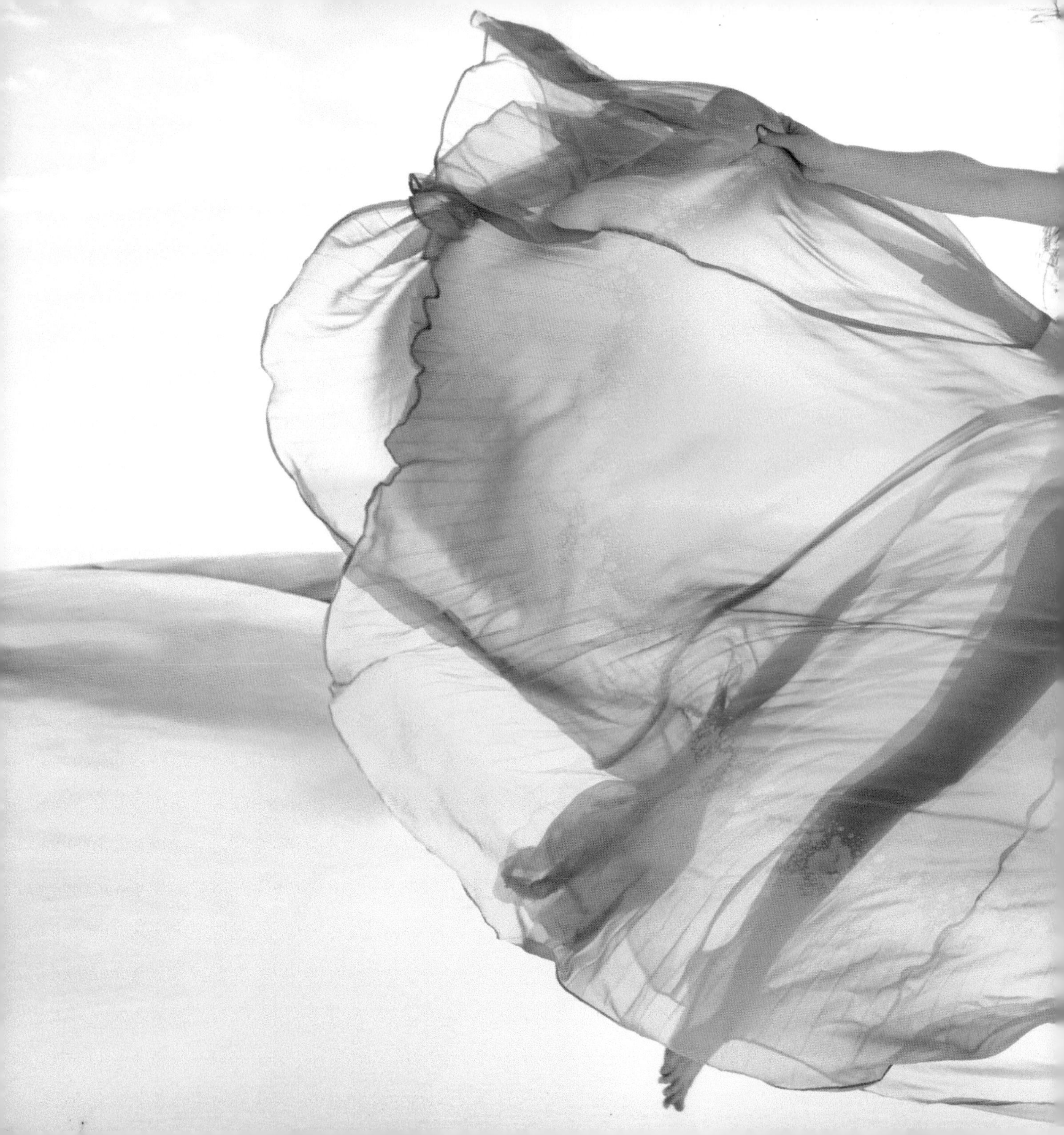

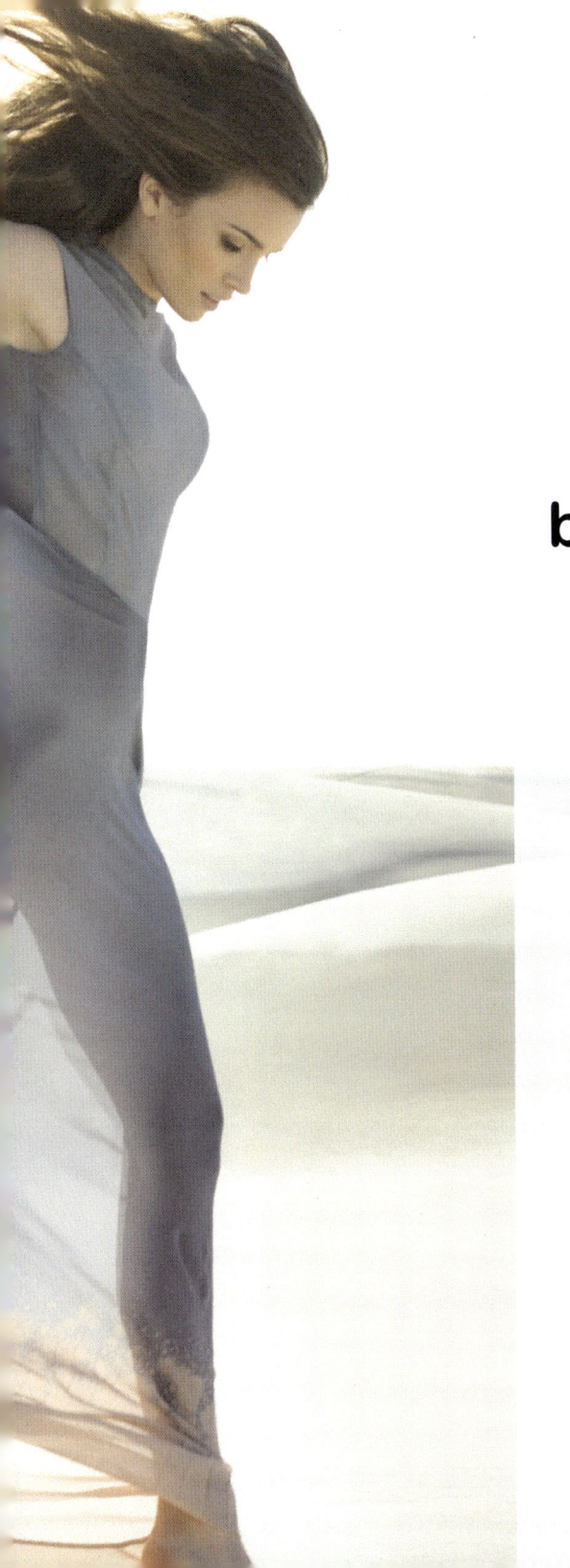

Global Winds. The spin of the Earth and the differences in temperature between the polar areas and the equator will produce global winds. These winds come in groups. These are the easterlies, westerlies, and trade winds. Trade winds are felt near the equator. As the Earth spins, the trade winds curve towards the west.

The westerly winds occur in the middle latitudes of the Earth. The westerlies blow towards the pole and from the west to the east. Easterlies winds blow away from the poles and from the north and south poles. These winds also curve east to west.

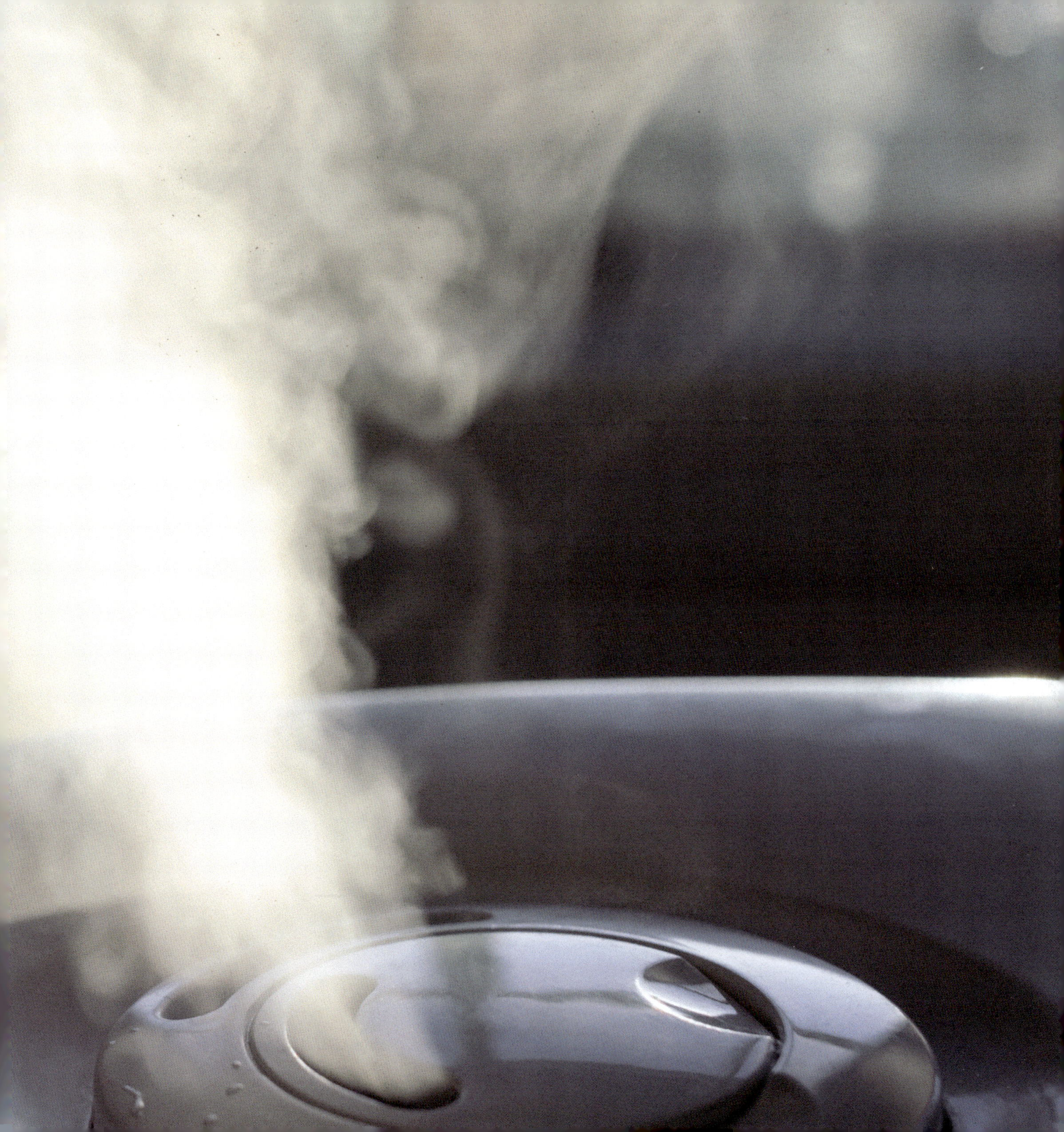

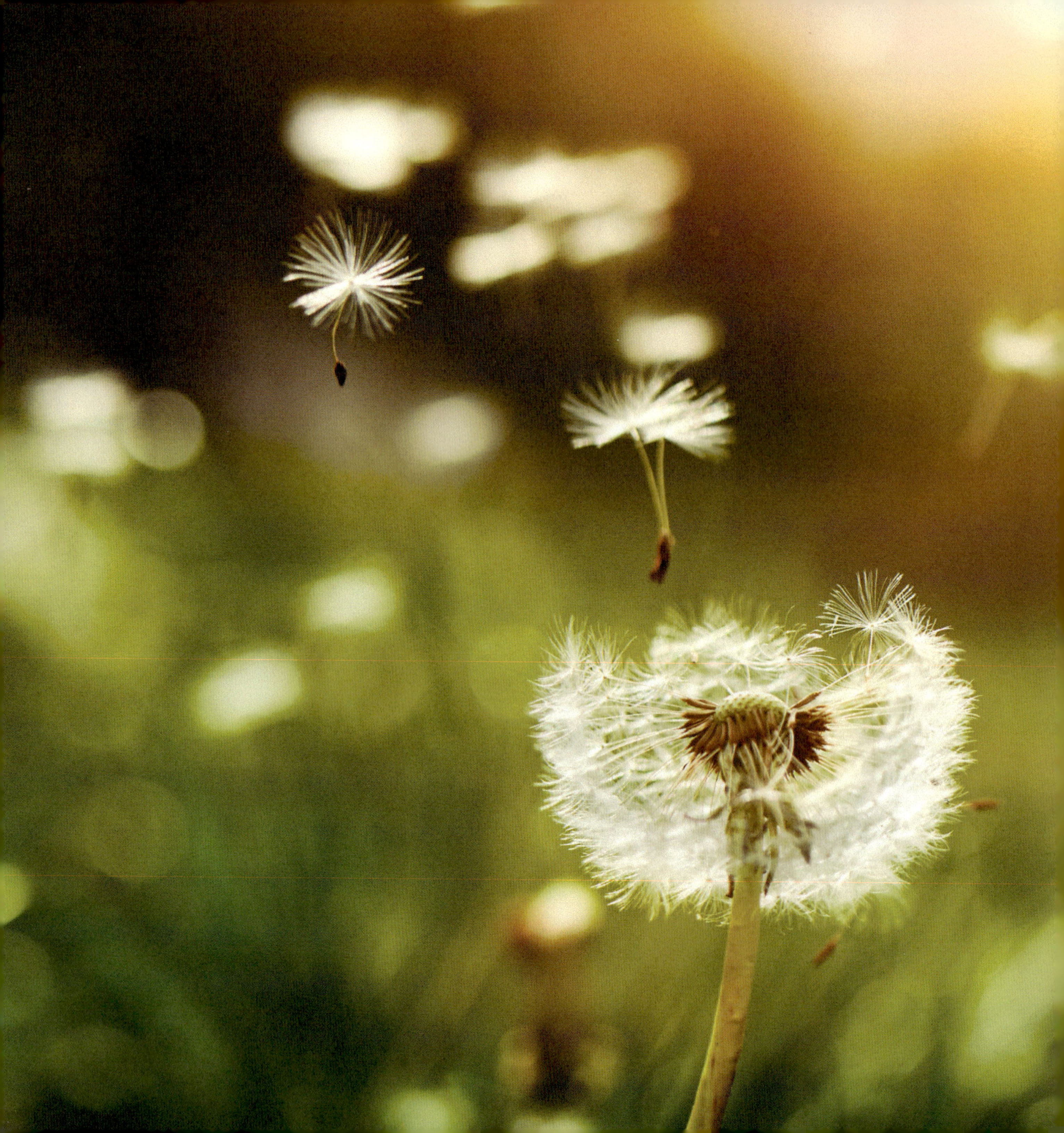

Local Winds. Local wind conditions are affected by land formations such as mountains and valleys. The changes in air pressure and temperatures locally will also generate some winds. These winds may change during the day. The wind that blows on the seashore from the ocean is an example of a local wind.

The uneven heating of the Earth's surface by the sun creates wind. This is due to some land elevations and water formations such as mountains, deserts, oceans, and lakes. In daytime, the air above the land heats up more quickly than the air over the ocean. By this, sea breeze is produced. At night, the air above the land will cool down faster than the ocean.

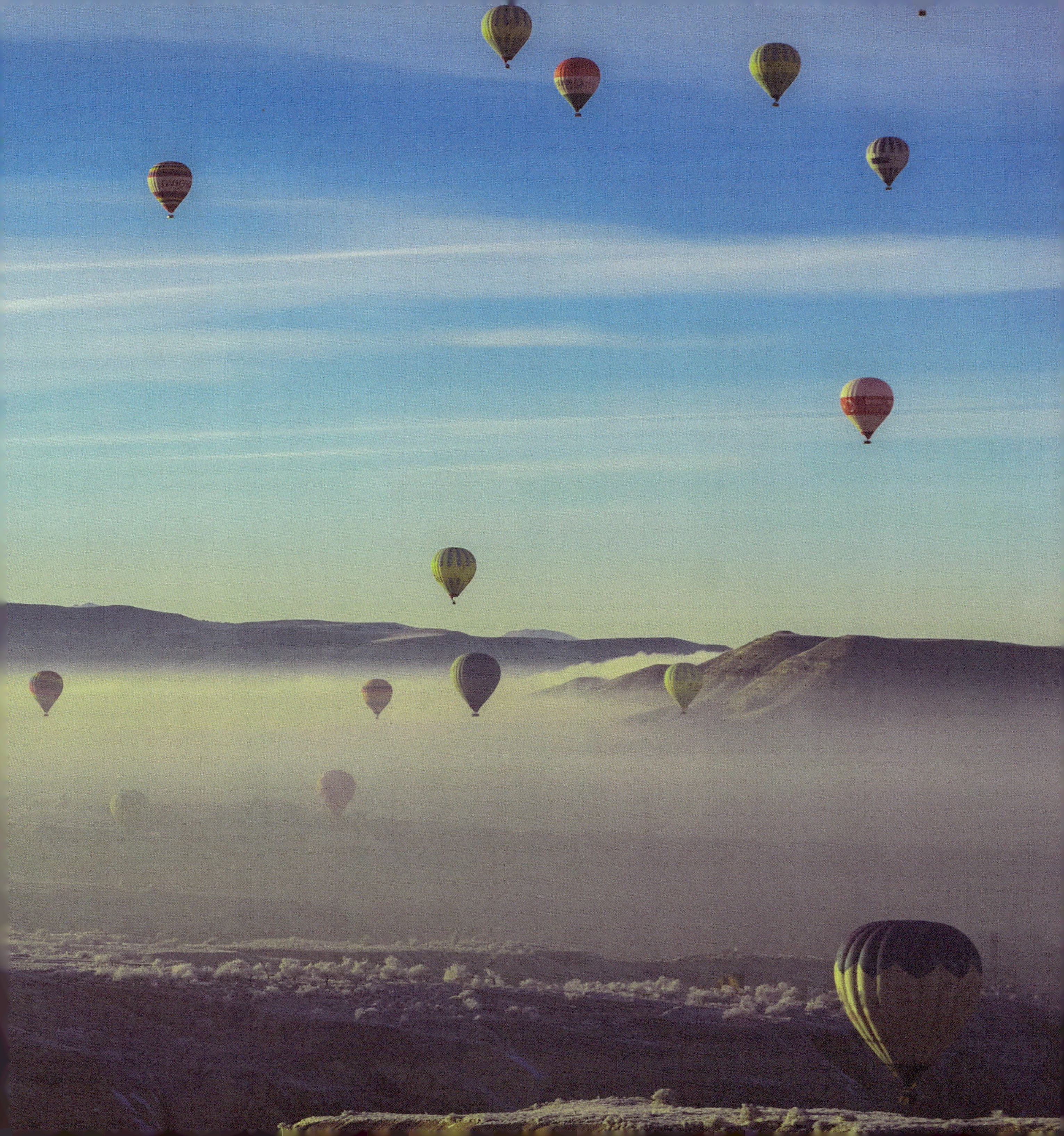

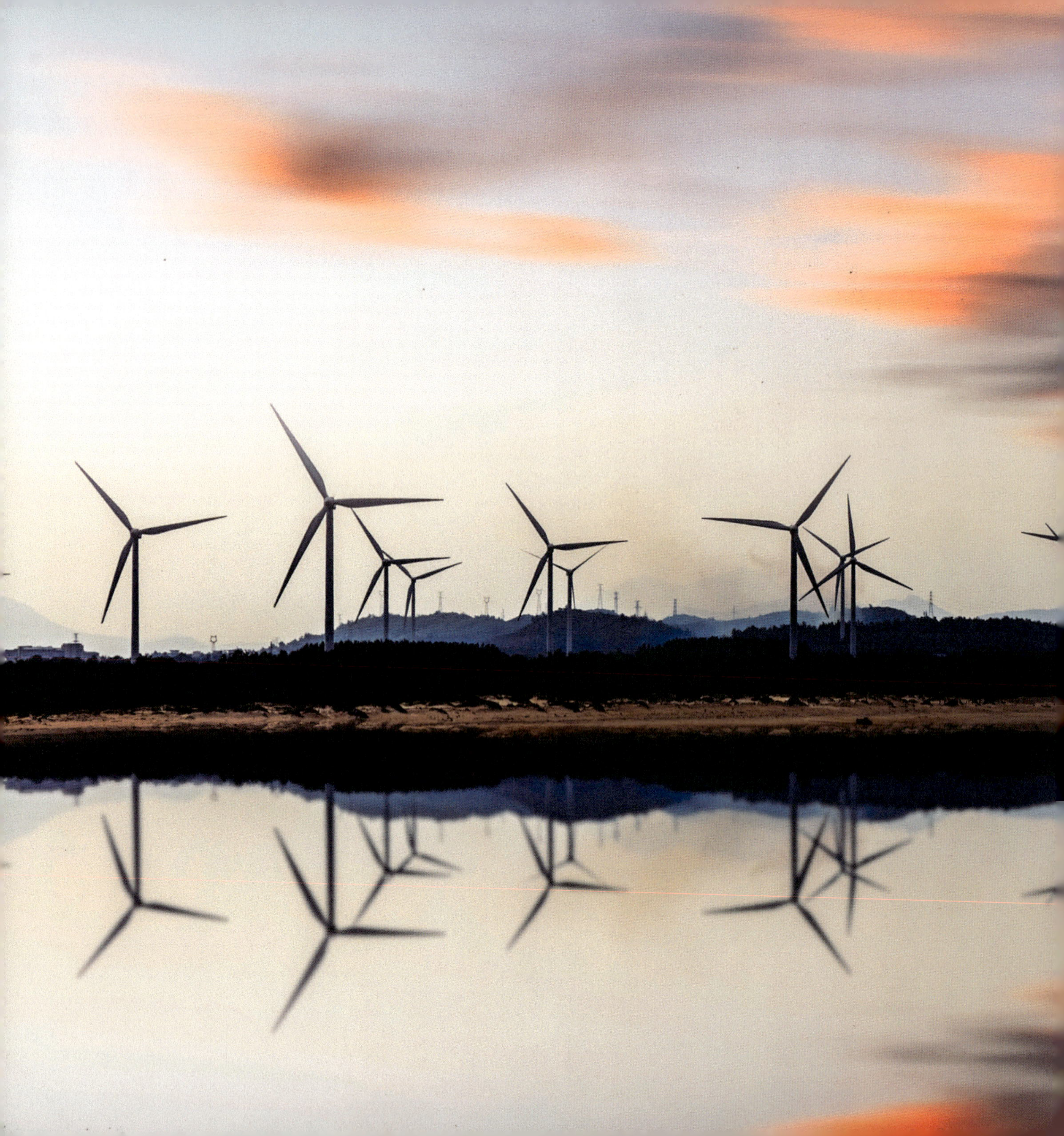

The layers of gases surrounding the Earth are referred to as air. As the air moves from high pressure areas to low pressure areas, wind is created.

Winds can be in the form of gale, hurricane, and breeze. Gusts are short bursts of wind moving at high speeds.

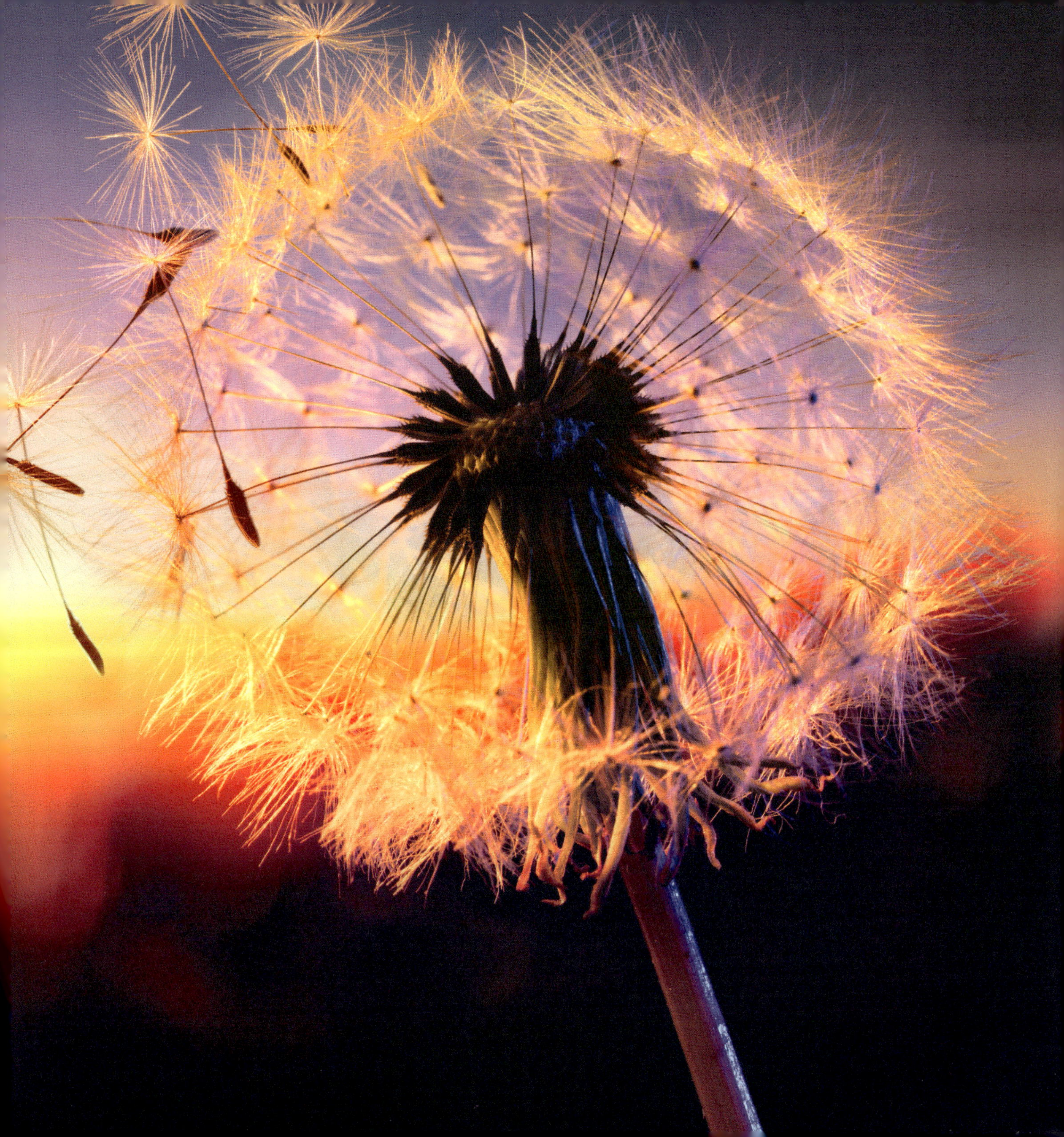

7 Bft

4 Bft

Wind speed is often measured by knots. Wind is used by sailing ships to power their movements.

Wind gives out wind energy which can be converted into wind power. It is a good source of electricity and it is renewable. Wind turbines, wind mills, and wind pumps are used to make wind energy conversions.

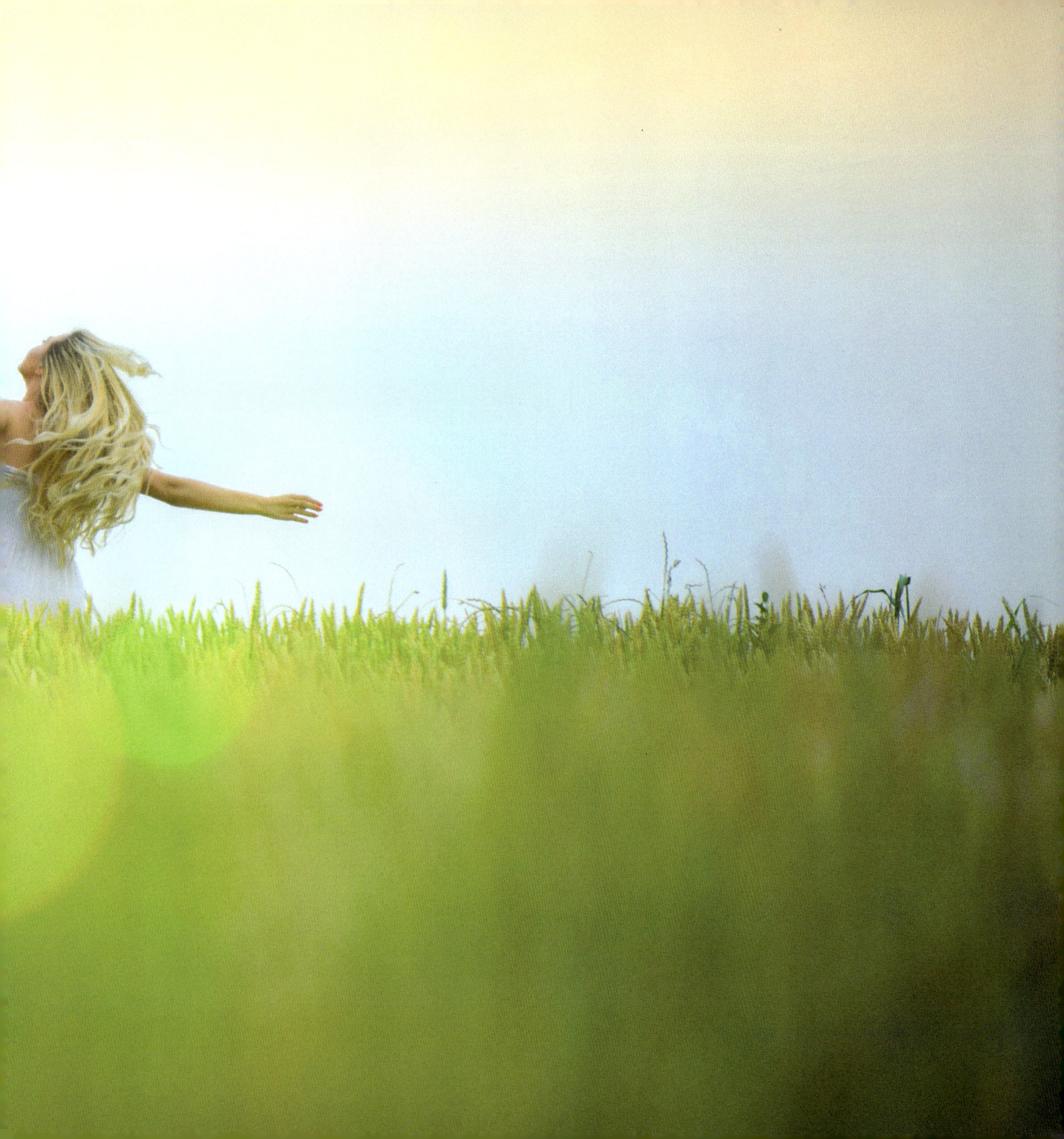

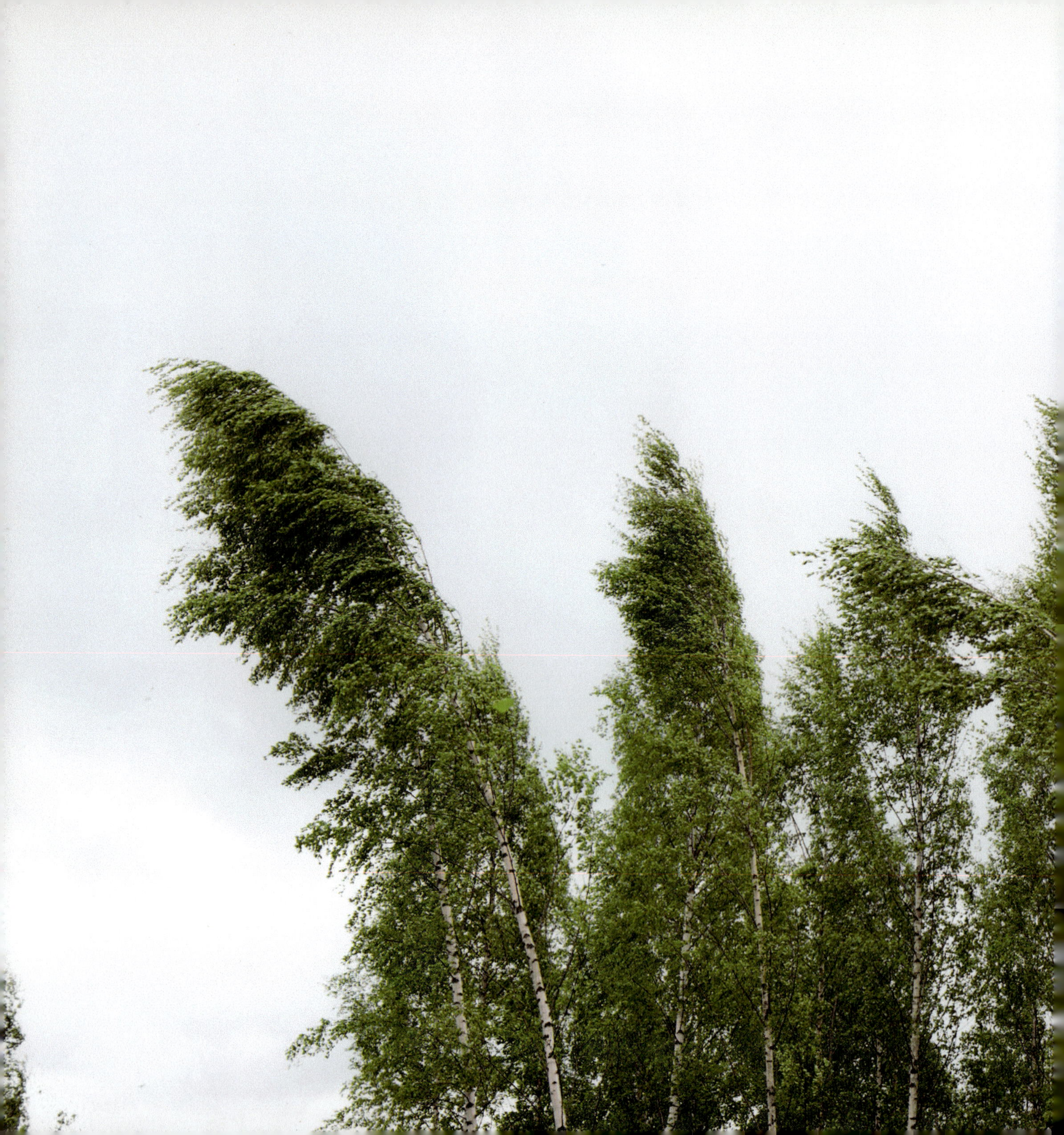

Do you love the windy days? How about the cool ocean breeze? This will surely make you feel fantastic. However, there are times that we feel restless because of the chilling breeze. Cold wind makes you tremble.

Wind is invisible and is free flowing. It's the air we breathe. It makes life on Earth possible. We should keep it clean to support our lives.

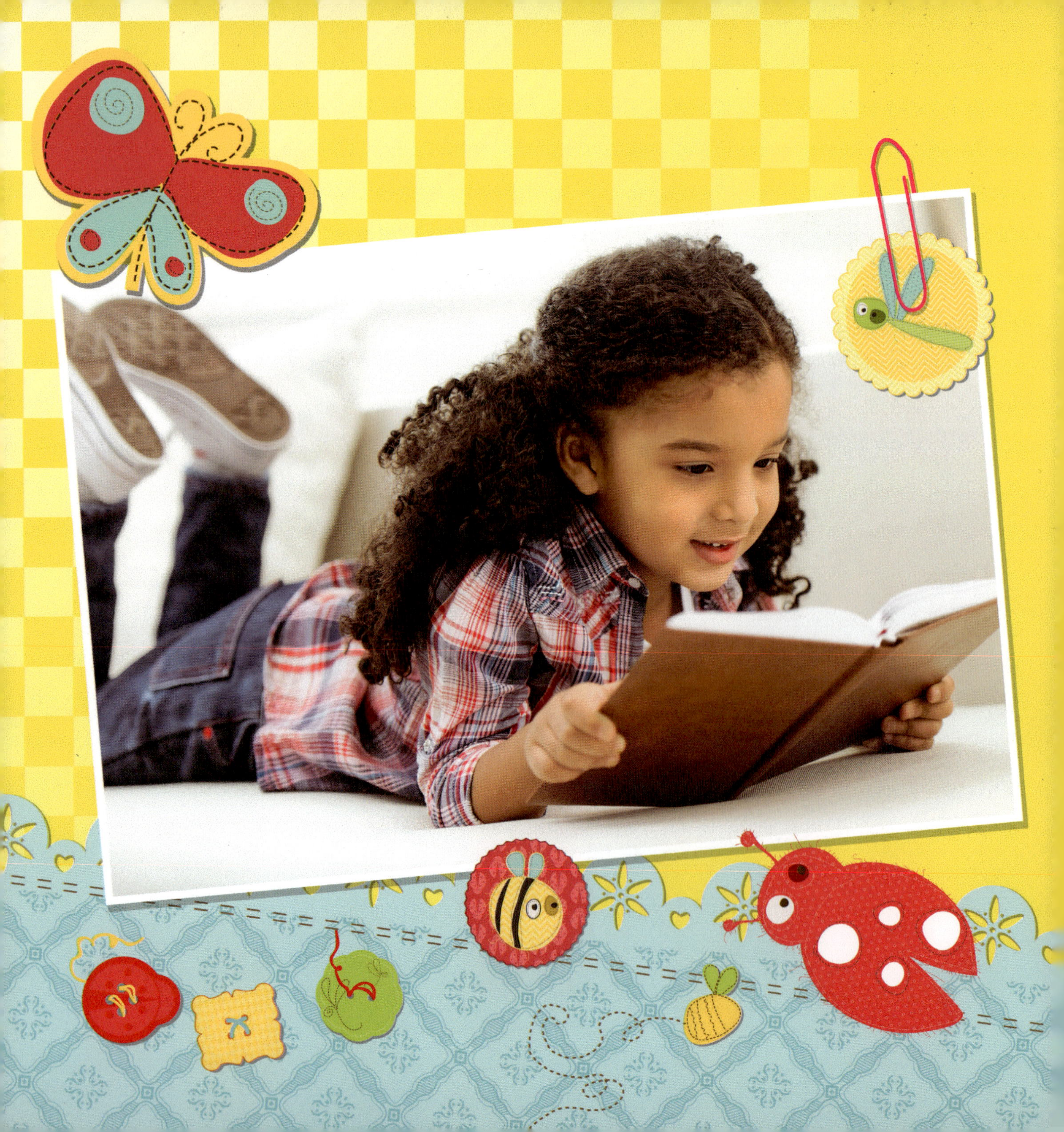